Mack Wilberg is the Music Director of the Mormon Tabernacle Choir. He was appointed Music Director in March of 2008, having served as Associate Music Director since May 1999. He is a former professor of music at Brigham Young University, where he received his bachelor's degree; his master's and doctoral degrees are from the University of Southern California.

In addition to his conducting responsibilities he is active as a pianist, choral clinician, composer, arranger, and guest conductor throughout the United States and abroad. In addition to the many compositions he has written for the Mormon Tabernacle Choir, his works have been performed by artists such as Renée Fleming, Frederica von Stade, Bryn Terfel, The King's Singers, and narrators Walter Cronkite and Claire Bloom.

Wilberg's arrangements and compositions are performed and recorded all over the world. With their grandeur, energy, and craftsmanship, they inspire performers and audiences everywhere.

'Mack Wilberg has emerged as one of the pre-eminent composers and arrangers of choral music in the United States today.'

Craig Jessop, Head of Music
Cain School of Arts, Utah State University

Have you tried?

Amazing grace!	(ISBN 978–0–19–337517–8)
Bound for the Promised Land	(ISBN 978–0–19–386917–2)
Deep River	(ISBN 978–0–19–386919–6)
I'm runnin' on	(ISBN 978–0–19–386987–5)
Shenandoah (SATB version)	(ISBN 978–0–19–386820–5)

OXFORD
UNIVERSITY PRESS

www.oup.com

ISBN 978–0–19–337518–5

9 780193 375185

FORD

SATB choir and piano four-hands

Mack Wilberg

Down to the River
to Pray

oxford sacred music

for the Timberline Middle School, Alpine, Utah,
Jennifer Halverson, Cathy Jolley, Kandis Taylor, conductors, Terry Hill, principal

Down to the River to Pray

Traditional American
arr. MACK WILBERG

A full score and set of parts for an orchestral accompaniment (picc, 2fl, 2ob, 2cl, 2bn, 4hn, 3tpt(C), 2tbn, btbn, tba, timp, 2perc (xylo, wood block), banjo (opt), str) is available on rental from the publisher's Hire Library or appropriate agent.

Recorded on *Come Thou Fount of Every Blessing: American Folk Hymns and Spirituals* (Mormon Tabernacle B001MYIPWS). Offprinted from Wilberg, *My Song in the Night* (ISBN 978–0–19–380499–9).

come on down, O, sis- ters, let's go down, down to the riv-er to

pray. O, sis- ters, let's go down, let's go down,

come on down, O, sis- ters, let's go down, down to the riv-er to

4

O, sis - ters, let's go down, let's go down,__ come on down,

O, sis - ters, let's go down, down to the riv-er to pray.

49 **T./B.** *unis.* ***mf***

As I went down to the riv-er to pray, stu-dy-in' a-bout that

52 good old__ way and who shall wear the robe and crown. Good Lord, show me the

56 way! O, bro-thers, let's go down, let's go down, come on down,

61 O, bro-thers, let's go down, down to the riv-er to pray.

O, fa-thers, let's go down, let's go down, come on down,

O, mo-thers, let's go down, down to the riv-er to pray.

8

SOPRANOS & ALTOS *unis.* **f**

As I went

TENORS & BASSES *unis.*

9

down to the riv-er to pray, stu-dy-in' a-bout that good old__ way and

who shall wear the robe and crown. Good Lord, show me the way!

12

down to the riv-er, down to the riv-er, down to the riv-er,

down to the riv-er, down to the riv-er, down to the riv-er,

down to the riv-er, down to the riv-er, down to the riv-er,

down to the riv-er, down to the riv-er, down to the riv-er,

down to the riv-er, down to the riv-er, down to the riv-er,

down to the riv-er, down to the riv-er, down to the riv-er,

down to the riv-er, down to the riv-er, down to the riv-er,

down to the riv-er, down to the riv-er, down to the riv-er,